BEGINNING SIGN LANGUAGE SERIES

# Holidays and Celebrations

Designed and illustrated by Jane Schneider and Kathy Kifer

Published by
Garlic Press
605 Powers Street
Eugene, OR 97402

www.garlicpress.com

ISBN 0-931993-10-5
Reorder Number GP-010

# TABLE OF CONTENTS

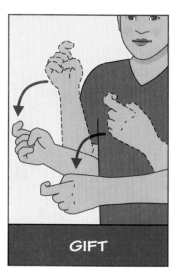

BIRTHDAY

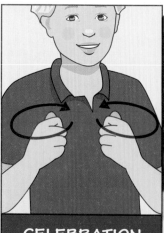

GIFT

CELEBRATION

# CELEBRATIONS

**VACATION**

**HOLIDAY**

$\mathcal{F}$ollow our calendar year of holidays and special occasions. Discover something new about the background of each. And learn signs which are important to each holiday and occasion.

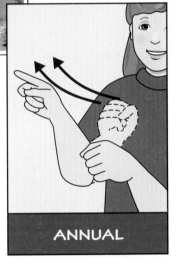

**ANNUAL**

**FESTIVAL**

**ANNIVERSARY**

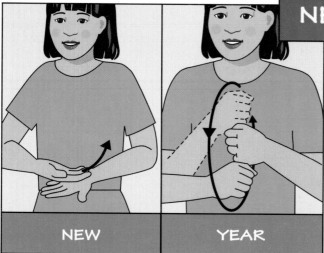

NEW

YEAR

The celebrations of New Year's Eve and New Year's Day mark the end of the old year and the beginning of the new year. The tradition of making noise and wearing costumes or silly hats probably comes from the ancient Roman midwinter festival of Janus—their god of beginnings and endings. Nowadays, people attend parties, make resolutions, and wish each other well.

EVE (evening)

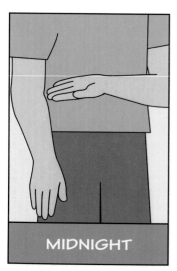

MIDNIGHT

**RESOLUTION**

**CONFETTI** (paper sprinkles)

**PARTY**

**TIME**

**VALENTINE'S** **DAY**

Nobody knows exactly why this very old holiday came to be celebrated but everybody knows it is a special day for sweethearts. Today, it is celebrated in honor of love. People exchange greeting cards called valentines, and small gifts—often chocolates and flowers.

**CUPID**

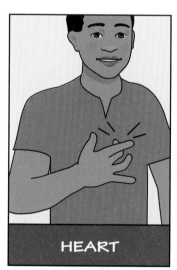

**HEART**

**LOVE**

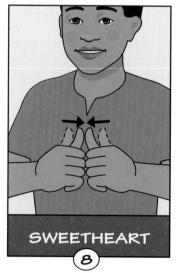

**SWEETHEART**

**FLOWERS**

# VALENTINE'S DAY
## FEBRUARY 14

**GREETING CARD** (greet + card)

**CHOCOLATES**

I love you!

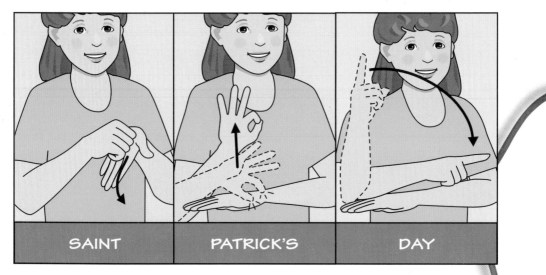

SAINT | PATRICK'S | DAY

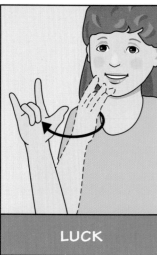

LUCK

SHAMROCK

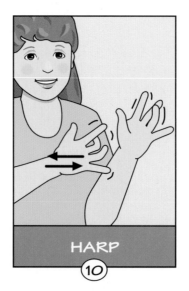

HARP

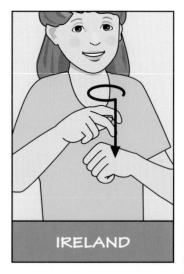

IRELAND

# St. PATRICK'S DAY

### March 17

In North America, Saint Patrick's Day is celebrated, especially by people of Irish ancestry, in remembrance of St.Patrick, the patron saint of Ireland. People dress in green to honor Ireland, the Emerald Isle. In many places there are parades, Irish music, and parties. And much green!

**RAINBOW**

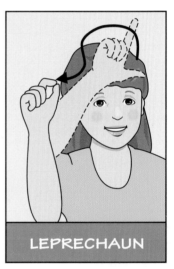

**LEPRECHAUN**

**POT**

**GOLD**

# EASTER

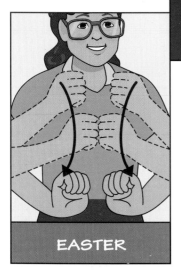

**EASTER**

Easter is celebrated on the first Sunday following the first full moon after March 21st. For Christians, it marks Jesus rising from the dead.

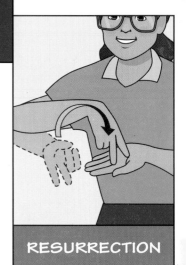

**RESURRECTION**

1

2

**BIBLE**

*Hallelujah, He has risen!*

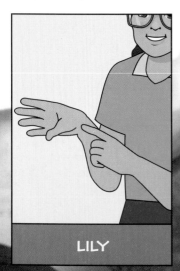

**LILY**

EGGS

EGG HUNT (search)

Although Easter is a religious holiday, some customs are older than Christianity: the bunnies and eggs are ancient symbols of spring and the beginning of new life.

CHICKS

BUNNY

# PASSOVER

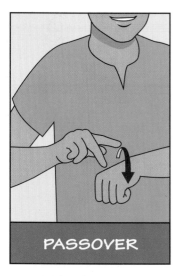

**PASSOVER**

Passover is a holiday celebrated by people of Jewish faith. It commemorates the freeing of the Jews from ancient Egypt. It is celebrated today with a Seder—a gathering of family and friends to pray, sing hymns, and eat together. Passover usually comes in April. It is one of the oldest celebrations of freedom in the world.

**CUSTOM**

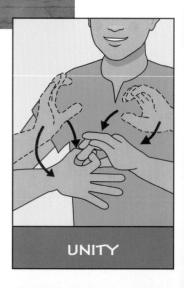

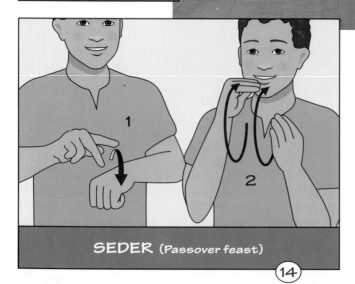

**SEDER** (Passover feast)

**UNITY**

# MOTHER'S DAY

Mother's Day and Father's Day are special days to honor our parents. Mother's Day began in 1914 and is celebrated the second Sunday in May. Father's Day, first celebrated in 1910, is the third Sunday in June.

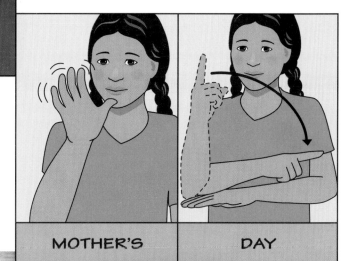

**MOTHER'S**  **DAY**

Traditionally, a red carnation is worn in honor of a living parent, while a white one is worn in remembrance of a parent who has died.

# FATHER'S DAY

**FATHER'S**  **DAY**

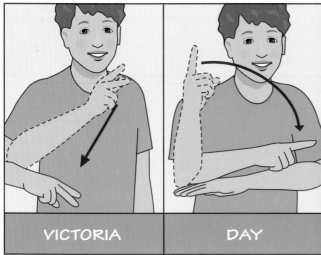

**VICTORIA**     **DAY**

Victoria Day is a Canadian holiday celebrated in remembrance of Victoria, who reigned as Queen of England 1837-1901. It is celebrated with fireworks and picnics on the Monday in May closest to the 24th. It is also the time many people plant their gardens.

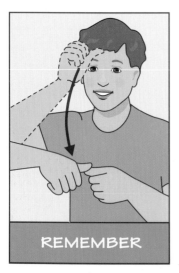

**REMEMBER**

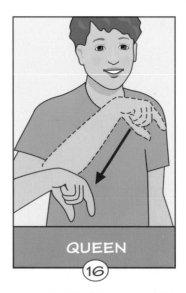

**QUEEN**

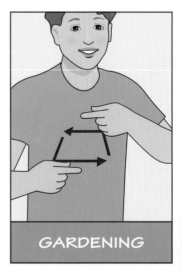

**GARDENING**

# MEMORIAL DAY

Memorial Day is a holiday celebrated in the United States on the last Monday of May. It is a day for remembering all the soldiers who lost their lives while serving in the military on behalf of the citizens of the country. The graves of soldiers are decorated with flags.

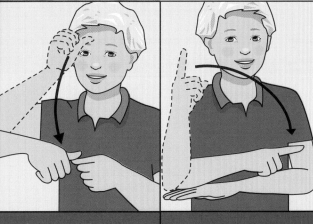

MEMORIAL

DAY

SOLDIER

CEMETERY

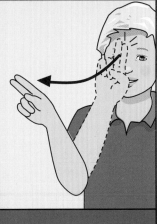

HONOR

# CANADA DAY
## July 1

CANADA

DAY

Canada Day celebrates the events of July 1st, 1867, when the British North America Act created the Canadian Federal Government. It is celebrated with fireworks, concerts and picnics.

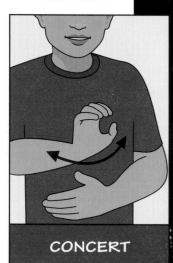

CONCERT

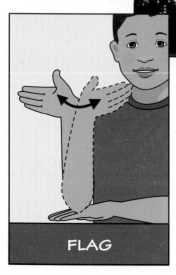

FLAG

PICNIC

# INDEPENDENCE DAY July 4

In America, Independence Day celebrates the events of July 4th, 1776, when the Declaration of Independence was signed by the Second Continental Congress, marking the beginning of the United States of America.

INDEPENDENCE

DAY

The Fourth of July, as it is also called, is celebrated with fireworks, parades, and picnics.

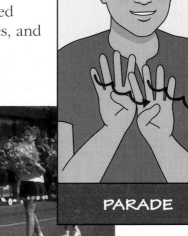

PARADE

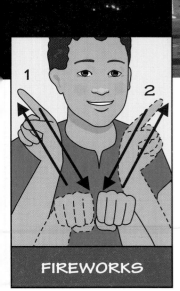

FIREWORKS

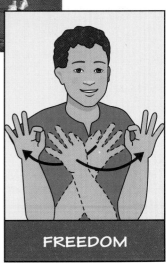

FREEDOM

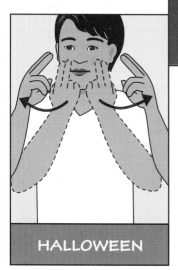

## HALLOWEEN
### October 31

**HALLOWEEN**

To the ancient Celtic people of the British Isles and northern France, this event was a time of fear and grief for the loss of the long days of sunlight. Today, Halloween has come to be a celebration of fun. Children dress in costumes to go house to house asking "Trick-or-Treat?" and collecting bags of candy.

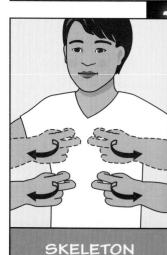

**JACK-O-LANTERN**

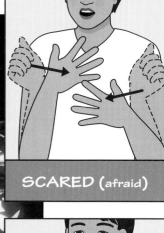

**SCARED (afraid)**

**SKELETON**

**GHOST**

COSTUME

MASK

TRICK

TREAT

21

# THANKSGIVING

THANKSGIVING    DAY

TURKEY    PUMPKIN    PIE

22

Thanksgiving is a special time for families and friends to gather together, give thanks and share a harvest celebration meal. In Canada it is celebrated the second Monday in October. In the United States it is celebrated the last Thursday in November.

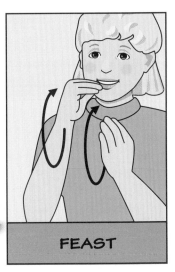

**FEAST**

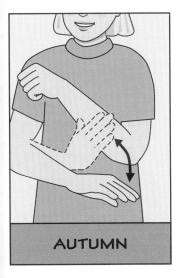

**AUTUMN**

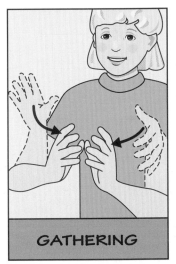

**GATHERING**

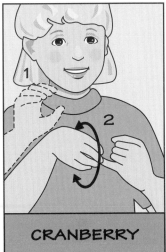

**CRANBERRY**

**CORN**

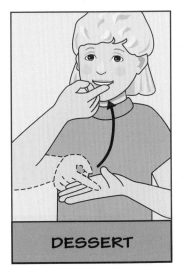

**DESSERT**

# HANUKKAH

**HANUKKAH**

**LAMP**

Hanukkah, an eight-day holiday, is a Festival of Lights. Remembering the biblical miracle of the temple lamp which burned for eight days and nights, one additional candle in the menorah is lit every evening as a prayer is sung. On the last night all of the candles are lit. Hanukkah comes in mid-winter, usually in December and is a season of gift giving and gatherings of family and friends.

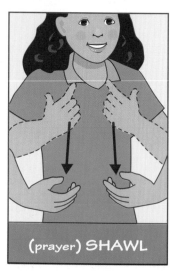

**PRAYER**

**(prayer) SHAWL**

COINS

DREIDEL

TEMPLE

MENORAH

**CHRISTMAS**

# CHRISTMAS
### December 25

**ORNAMENT**

**JESUS**

For Christians, Christmas celebrates the birth of Jesus, the Christ child. Also, Christmas celebrations have become a combination of traditions from around the world. It is a time for family gatherings, exchanging of gifts, and singing of carols. People decorate their homes inside and out using lights, holly, evergreen branches, and a tree dressed in ornaments.

1  2

**BETHLEHEM**

**ANGEL**

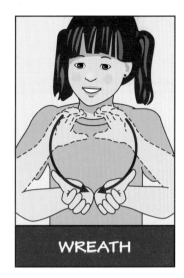

**WREATH**

**STOCKINGS**

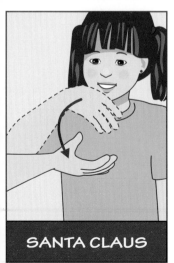

**SANTA CLAUS**

**TOY**

**REINDEER**

**KWANZAA**

Kwanzaa, established in 1966, is an African-American festival. Families celebrate the joy of the African harvest and culture, shared memories, shared beliefs, and *Nguzo Saba*, the seven principles of Kwanzaa—Unity, Self-determination, Working together, Sharing profit, Purpose, Creativity, and Faith.

**COMMUNITY**

**BEADS**

**BASKET**

**FRUIT**

ANCESTORS

AFRICAN-AMERICAN

FAMILY

CANDLES

# LAS POSADAS
## December 16-24

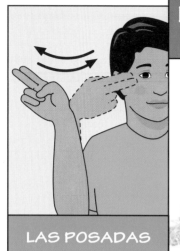

**LAS POSADAS**

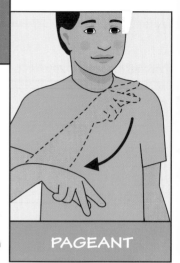

**PAGEANT**

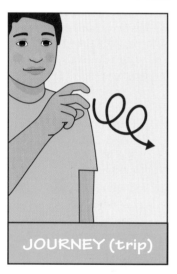

**JOURNEY (trip)**

Children act out the story of Jesus' birth by going as Mary and Joseph from house to house to look for shelter, or *posada*. A party is held at a different house every night for the nine nights before Christmas. Sometimes there is a *piñata* filled with candy and toys. There is music and everyone has fun. People decorate the *nacimiento,* or manger scene, and say *"Feliz Navidad,"* which in Spanish means Merry Christmas!

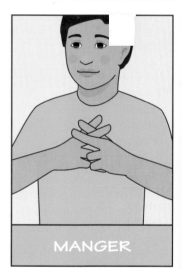

**MANGER**

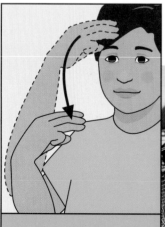

**MARY (biblical)**

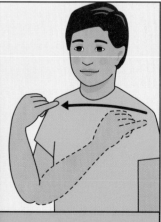

**JOSEPH (biblical)**

# INDEX OF SIGNS

# Also from Garlic Press

## Finger Alphabet GP-046
Uses word games and activities to teach the finger alphabet.

## Signing in School GP-047
Presents signs needed in a school setting.

## Can I Help? Helping the Hearing Impaired in Emergency Situations
GP-057 Signs, sentences and information to help communicate with the hearing impaired.

## Caring for Young Children: Signing for Day Care Providers and Sitters
GP-058 Signs for feelings, directions, activities and foods, bedtime, discipline and comfort-giving.

## An Alphabet of Animal Signs
GP-065 Animal illustrations and associated signs for each letter of the alphabet.

## Mother Goose in Sign
GP-066 Fully illustrated nursery rhymes.

## Number and Letter Games
GP-072 Presents a variety of games involving the finger alphabet and sign numbers.

## Expanded Songs in Sign
GP-005 Eleven songs in Signed English. The easy-to-follow illustrations enable you to sign along.

## Foods GP-087
A colorful collection of photos with signs for 43 common foods.

## Fruits & Vegetables GP-088
Thirty-nine beautiful photos with signs.

## Pets, Animals & Creatures
GP-089 Seventy-seven photos with signs of pets, animals & creatures familiar to signers of all ages.

## Signing at Church
GP-098 For adults and young adults. Helpful phrases, the Lord's Prayer and *John 3:16*.

## Signing at Sunday School
GP-099 Phrases, songs, Bible verses and the story of Jesus clearly illustrated.

## Family and Community
GP-073 Signs for relationships and family and community members in their job roles.

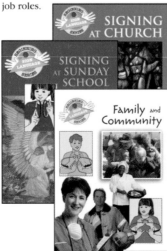

## Coyote & Bobcat
GP-081 A Navajo story serving to tell how Coyote and Bobcat got their shapes.

## Raven & Water Monster
GP-082 This Haida story tells how Raven gained his beautiful black color and how he brought water to the earth.

## Fountain of Youth
GP-086 This Korean folk tale about neighbors shows the rewards of kindness and the folly of greed.

## Ananse the Spider: Why Spiders Stay on the Ceiling
GP-085 A West African folk tale about the boastful spider Ananse and why he now hides in dark corners.

www.garlicpress.com